RUBANK EDUCATIONAL LIBRARY No. 142

Advanced Method

Eb OR BBb BASS

VOL. I

WM. GOWER
AND
H. VOXMAN

AN OUTLINED COURSE OF STUDY
DESIGNED TO FOLLOW UP ANY
OF THE VARIOUS ELEMENTARY
AND INTERMEDIATE METHODS

RUBANK®

HAL•LEONARD®
CORPORATION
7777 W. BLUEMOUND RD. P.O. BOX 13819 MILWAUKEE, WI 53213

NOTE

THE RUBANK ADVANCED METHOD for E♭ or BB♭ Bass is published in two volumes, the course of study being divided in the following manner:

Vol. I
{ Keys of B♭, E♭, F, A♭, and C Major.
{ Keys of G, C, D, F, and A Minor.

Vol. II
{ Keys of D♭, G, G♭, D, C♭, and A Major.
{ Keys of B♭, E, E♭, and B Minor.

PREFACE

THIS METHOD is designed to follow any of the various Elementary and Intermediate instruction series, or Elementary instruction series comprising two or more volumes, depending upon the previous development of the student. The authors have found it necessary in their teaching experience to draw from many sources in order to provide a progressive course of study. The present publication assembles in two volumes, the material essential to a well-rounded musical development.

THE OUTLINES, one of which is included in each of the respective volumes, tend to afford an objective picture of the student's progress. They will facilitate the ranking of members in a large ensemble or they may serve as a basis for awards of merit. In addition, a one-sided development along strictly technical or strictly melodic lines is avoided. The use of these outlines, however, is not imperative and they may be discarded at the discretion of the teacher.

Wm. Gower — H. Voxman

PRACTICE AND GRADE REPORT

SECOND SEMESTER

Student's Name _____

Date _____

Week	Sun.	Mon.	Tue.	Wed.	Thu.	Fri.	Sat.	Total	Parent's Signature	Grade
1										
2										
3										
4										
5										
6										
7										
8										
9										
10										
11										
12										
13										
14										
15										
16										
17										
18										
19										
20										

Semester Grade _____

Instructor's Signature _____

FIRST SEMESTER

Student's Name _____

Date _____

Week	Sun.	Mon.	Tue.	Wed.	Thu.	Fri.	Sat.	Total	Parent's Signature	Grade
1										
2										
3										
4										
5										
6										
7										
8										
9										
10										
11										
12										
13										
14										
15										
16										
17										
18										
19										
20										

Semester Grade _____

Instructor's Signature _____

Chromatic Fingering Chart for BBb Bass

① The B♮ or C♭ below the staff is too sharp. Flatten this tone enough to make it in good tune.

② The C on the second space is usually too flat. Correct this in slow passages by using 1st and 3rd valves.

③ The D on the third line will sometimes be too flat. Use 1st and 2nd valves to improve this in slow passages.

TABLE OF HARMONICS

Copyright MCMLI by Rubank, Inc., Chicago, Ill.
International Copyright Secured

Chromatic Fingering Chart for E♭ Bass

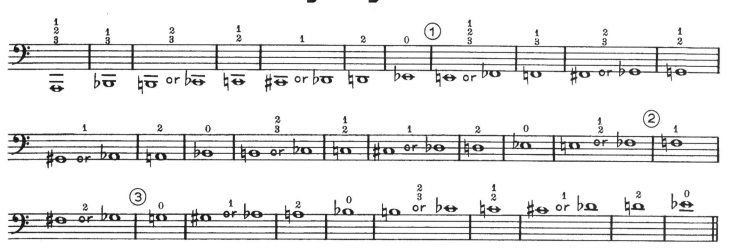

① The E♮ or F♭ below the staff is too sharp. Flatten this tone enough to make it in good tune.

② The F on the fourth line is usually too flat. Correct this in slow passages by using 1st and 3rd valves.

③ The G on the fourth space will sometimes be too flat. Use 1st and 2nd valves to improve this in slow passages.

TABLE OF HARMONICS

Fingerings for the tones above high E♭:

OUTLINE
OF
RUBANK ADVANCED METHOD
FOR
BB♭ BASS, Vol. I
BY
Wm. Gower and H. Voxman

UNIT	SCALES and ARPEGGIOS	(Key)	MELODIC INTERPRETATION	ARTICULATION	FLEXIBILITY EXERCISES	ORNAMENTS	SOLOS	UNIT COMPLETED
1	8 (1) 9 (5)	B♭	26 (1)	45 (1)	57 (1)	63 (1)	69 (1)	
2	8 (2) 9 (6)	B♭	26 (2)	45 (2)	57 (1)	63 (1)	69 (1)	
3	8 (3) 9 (7)	B♭	27 (3)	46 (3)	57 (2)	63 (2)	69 (1)	
4	9 (4) (8)	B♭	28 (4)	46 (4)	57 (2)	63 (3)	69 (1)	
5	10 (9)	g	28 (5)	46 (5)	57 (3)	63 (4)	69 (1)	
6	10 (10) (13)	g	29 (6)	47 (6)	57 (3)	63 (5)	69 (1)	
7	10 (12)	g	29 (7)	47 (7)	57 (4)	64 (6)	69 (2)	
8	11 (14) (15) (16)	g	30 (8)	47 (7)	57 (4)	64 (7)	69 (2)	
9	11 (17) 12 (21)	E♭	30 (9)	47 (8)	57 (5)	64 (8)	69 (2)	
10	11 (18) 12 (22)	E♭	31 (10)	48 (9)	57 (5)	64 (9)	69 (2)	
11	12 (19) (23)	E♭	31 (11)	48 (9)	57 (6)	64 (9)	69 (2)	
12	12 (20)	E♭	32 (12)	48 (10)	57 (6)	65 (10)	69 (2)	
13	12 (24) 13 (26)	c	32 (13)	49 (11)	57 (7)	65 (10)	70 (3)	
14	13 (25)	c	33 (14)	49 (12)	57 (7)	65 (11)	70 (3)	
15	13 (27) (28) (29)	c	34 (15)	49 (13)	58 (8)	65 (12)	70 (3)	
16	14 (30) 15 (34)	F	34 (16)	50 (14)	58 (8)	65 (13)	70 (3)	
17	14 (31) 15 (35)	F	35 (17)	50 (15)	58 (9)	65 (14)	70 (3)	
18	14 (32) 15 (37)	F	35 (18)	50 (15)	58 (9)	65 (15)	70 (3)	
19	14 (33) 15 (38)	F	36 (19)	50 (16)	58 (9)	66 (16)	70 (4)	
20	16 (39)	d	36 (20)	51 (17)	58 (10)	66 (17)	70 (4)	
21	16 (40)	d	37 (21)	51 (18)	58 (10)	66 (18) (19)	70 (4)	
22	16 (41) (42) (43)	d	38 (22)	52 (19)	58 (10)	66 (20)	70 (4)	
23	17 (44) 19 (52)	A♭	38 (23)	52 (20)	59 (11)	66 (21)	70 (4)	
24	17 (46) 19 (53)	A♭	38 (24)	52 (20)	59 (11)	66 (22)	70 (4)	
25	18 (48) 19 (54)	A♭	39 (25)	53 (22)	59 (12)	67 (23)	71 (5)	
26	18 (50)	A♭	39 (25)	53 (23)	59 (12)	67 (24)	71 (5)	
27	20 (55) 21 (60)	f	40 (26)	54 (24)	59 (13)	67 (25)	71 (5)	
28	20 (56) 22 (62)	f	40 (27)	54 (25)	59 (13)	68 (26)	71 (5)	
29	20 (58) 22 (64)	f	40 (27)	54 (25)	59 (14)	68 (26)	71 (5)	
30	22 (65) 24 (71)	C	41 (28)	54 (26)	59 (14)	68 (27)	71 (5)	
31	22 (66) 24 (72)	C	42 (29)	55 (27)	59 (15)	68 (27)	72 (6)	
32	23 (68) 24 (73)	C	42 (30)	55 (28)	59 (15)	68 (28)	72 (6)	
33	24 (70) (74)	C	43 (31)	56 (29)	59 (15)	68 (29)	72 (6)	
34	25 (75)	a	43 (32)	56 (30)	59 (15)	68 (30)	72 (6)	
35	25 (76)	a	44 (33)	56 (31)	59 (16)	68 (31)	72 (6)	
36	25 (77) (78) (79)	a	44 (33)	56 (31)	59 (16)	68 (32)	72 (6)	

NUMERALS designate page number.
ENCIRCLED NUMERALS designate exercise number.
COMPLETED EXERCISES may be indicated by crossing out the rings, thus, ⊗.

OUTLINE
OF
RUBANK ADVANCED METHOD
FOR
E♭ BASS, Vol. I
BY
Wm. Gower and H. Voxman

UNIT	SCALES and ARPEGGIOS	(Key)	MELODIC INTERPRETATION	ARTICULATION	FLEXIBILITY EXERCISES	ORNAMENTS	SOLOS	UNIT COMPLETED
1	8 ① 9 ⑤	B♭	26 ①	45 ①	60 ①	63 ①	69 ①	
2	8 ② 9 ⑥	B♭	26 ②	45 ②	60 ①	63 ①	69 ①	
3	8 ③ 9 ⑦	B♭	27 ③	46 ③	60 ②	63 ②	69 ①	
4	9 ④ ⑧	B♭	28 ④	46 ④	60 ②	63 ③	69 ①	
5	10 ⑨	g	28 ⑤	46 ⑤	60 ③	63 ④	69 ①	
6	10 ⑪ ⑬	g	29 ⑥	47 ⑥	60 ③	63 ⑤	69 ①	
7	10 ⑫	g	29 ⑦	47 ⑦	60 ④	64 ⑥	69 ②	
8	11 ⑭ ⑮ ⑯	g	30 ⑧	47 ⑦	60 ④	64 ⑦	69 ②	
9	11 ⑰ 12 ㉑	E♭	30 ⑨	47 ⑧	60 ⑤	64 ⑧	69 ②	
10	11 ⑱ 12 ㉒	E♭	31 ⑩	48 ⑨	60 ⑤	64 ⑨	69 ②	
11	12 ⑲ ㉓	E♭	31 ⑪	48 ⑨	60 ⑥	64 ⑨	69 ②	
12	12 ⑳	E♭	32 ⑫	48 ⑩	60 ⑥	65 ⑩	69 ②	
13	12 ㉔ 13 ㉖	c	32 ⑬	49 ⑪	60 ⑦	65 ⑩	70 ③	
14	13 ㉕	c	33 ⑭	49 ⑫	60 ⑦	65 ⑪	70 ③	
15	13 ㉗ ㉘ ㉙	c	34 ⑮	49 ⑬	61 ⑧	65 ⑫	70 ③	
16	14 ㉚ 15 ㉞	F	34 ⑯	50 ⑭	61 ⑧	65 ⑬	70 ③	
17	14 ㉛ 15 ㊱	F	35 ⑰	50 ⑮	61 ⑨	65 ⑭	70 ③	
18	14 ㉜ 15 ㊲	F	35 ⑱	50 ⑮	61 ⑨	65 ⑮	70 ③	
19	14 ㉝ 15 ㊳	F	36 ⑲	50 ⑯	61 ⑨	66 ⑯	70 ④	
20	16 ㊴	d	36 ⑳	51 ⑰	61 ⑩	66 ⑰	70 ④	
21	16 ㊵	d	37 ㉑	51 ⑱	61 ⑩	66 ⑱ ⑲	70 ④	
22	16 ㊶ ㊷ ㊸	d	38 ㉒	52 ⑲	61 ⑩	66 ⑳	70 ④	
23	17 ㊺ 19 (52)	A♭	38 ㉓	52 ㉑	62 ⑪	66 ㉑	70 ④	
24	18 ㊼ 19 (53)	A♭	38 ㉔	52 ㉑	62 ⑪	66 ㉒	70 ④	
25	18 ㊾ 19 (54)	A♭	39 ㉕	53 ㉒	62 ⑫	67 ㉓	71 ⑤	
26	19 (51)	A♭	39 ㉕	53 ㉓	62 ⑫	67 ㉔	71 ⑤	
27	20 (55) 21 (61)	f	40 ㉖	54 ㉔	62 ⑬	67 ㉕	71 ⑤	
28	20 (57) 22 (63)	f	40 ㉗	54 ㉕	62 ⑬	68 ㉖	71 ⑤	
29	21 (59) 22 (64)	f	40 ㉗	54 ㉕	62 ⑭	68 ㉖	71 ⑤	
30	22 (65) 24 (71)	C	41 ㉘	54 ㉖	62 ⑭	68 ㉗	71 ⑤	
31	23 (67) 24 (72)	C	42 ㉙	55 ㉗	62 ⑮	68 ㉗	72 ⑥	
32	23 (69) 24 (73)	C	42 ㉚	55 ㉘	62 ⑮	68 ㉘	72 ⑥	
33	24 (70) (74)	C	43 ㉛	56 ㉙	62 ⑮	68 ㉙	72 ⑥	
34	25 (75)	a	43 ㉜	56 ㉚	62 ⑮	68 ㉚	72 ⑥	
35	25 (76)	a	44 ㉝	56 ㉛	62 ⑯	68 ㉛	72 ⑥	
36	25 (77) (78) (79)	a	44 ㉝	56 ㉛	62 ⑯	68 ㉜	72 ⑥	

NUMERALS designate page number.
ENCIRCLED NUMERALS designate exercise number.
COMPLETED EXERCISES may be indicated by crossing out the rings, thus, ⊗.

Scales and Arpeggios
Bb Major

Various articulations may be used in the chromatic, the interval and the chord studies at the instructor's option.

G Minor

The sign ∧ indicates a half-step

12

F Major

D Minor

F Minor

A Minor

Studies in Melodic Interpretation

The following studies are designed to aid in the development of the student's interpretative ability. Careful attention to the marks of expression is essential to effective use of the material. Pencil the technically difficult passages and devote extra time to their mastery.

In rhythmic music of the more rapid tempi (marches, dances, etc.) tones that are equal divisions of the beat are played somewhat detached (staccato). Tones that equal a beat or are multiples of a beat are held full value. Tones followed by rests are usually held full value. The latter point should be observed in slow music particularly.

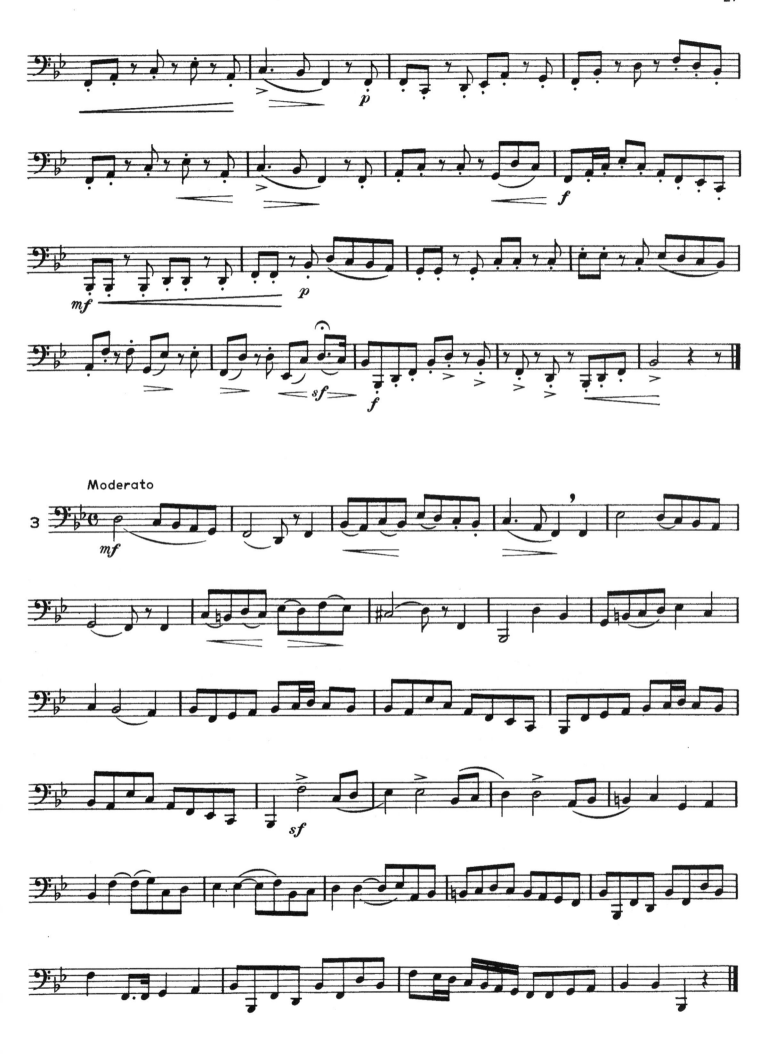

GATTI

Allegretto

4

Poco meno

Tempo I

WEISSENBORN

Allegro

5

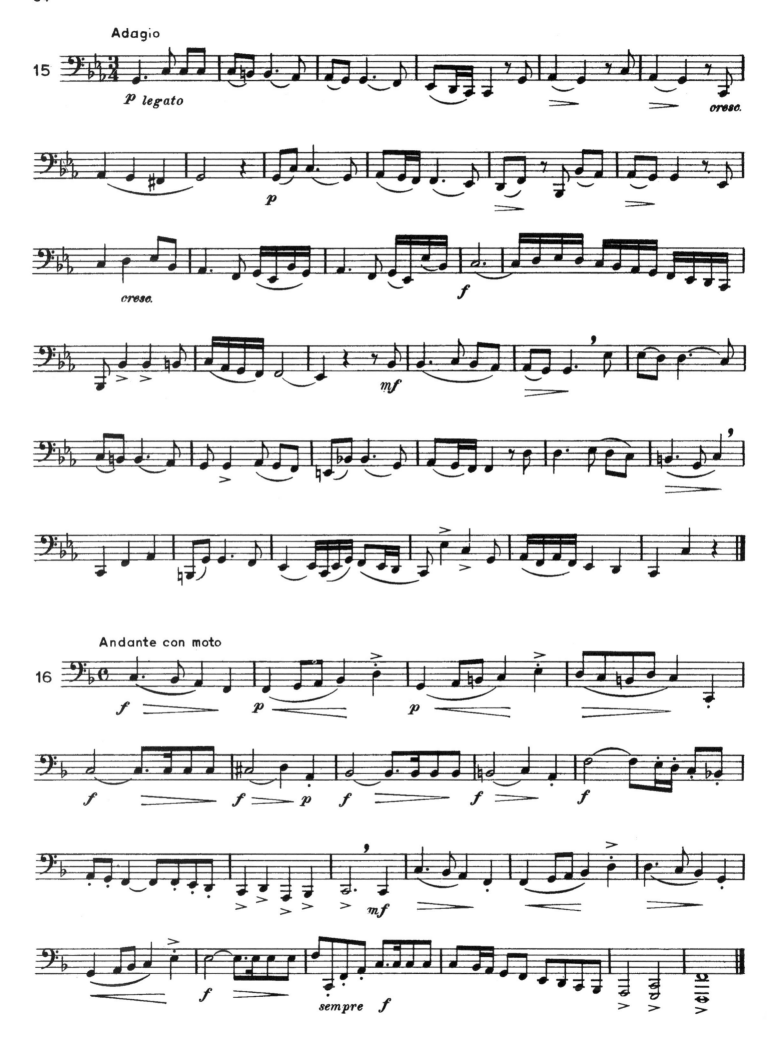

MOZART

Marcia funebre

21

MUSETTE

BACH

40

GALOP

Studies in Articulation

In all exercises where no tempo is indicated the student should play the study as rapidly as is consistent with tonal control and technical accuracy. The first practice on each exercise should be done very slowly in order that the articulation may be carefully observed.

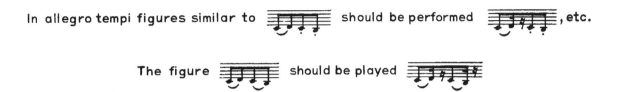

The figure ♪♪♪♪ should be played ♪♪♪♪

48

Allegro moderato

Practice No.17 with various articulations.

19

Practice No. 20 with various articulations.

20 *BBb Bass only*

sempre staccato

21 *Eb Bass only*

54

56

Flexibility Exercises for BB♭ Bass

Keep the tone well sustained throughout the slur indicated, leaving no gaps between the tones. The slur must be made smoothly and evenly by the flexibility of the embouchure.

Adhere strictly to the fingerings given.

Flexibility Exercises for BBb Bass (Cont'd)

Flexibility Exercises for E♭ Bass

Keep the tone well sustained throughout the slur indicated, leaving no gaps between the tones. The slur must be made smoothly and evenly by the flexibility of the embouchure.

Adhere strictly to the fingerings given.

Musical Ornamentation (Embellishments)

The following treatment of ornamentation is by no means complete. It is presented here only as a guide to the execution of those ornaments which the student may encounter at this stage of his musical development. There are different manners of performing the same ornament.

The Trill (Shake)

The trill (or shake) consists of the rapid alternation of two tones. They are represented by the printed note (called the principal note) and the next tone above in the diatonic scale. The interval between the two tones may be either a half-step or a whole-step. The signs for the trill are *tr* and ⌇⌇.

An accidental when used in conjunction with the trill sign affects the upper note of the trill.

Fingerings above refer to Eb Bass; fingerings below refer to BBb Bass.

Grace Notes (Appoggiatura)

The grace notes are indicated by notes of a smaller size. They may be divided into two classes: long and short.

Long grace notes

from "Serenade" Haydn

In instrumental music of recent composition the short grace notes should occupy as little time as possible and that value is taken preceding the principal note. They may be single, double, triple or quadruple, as the case may be. The single short grace note is printed as a small eighth note with a stroke through its hook. It is not to be accented. Use trill fingerings when fundamental fingerings are too difficult.

Short grace notes

The Mordent

The short mordent (♦) consists of a single rapid alternation of the principal note with its lower auxiliary. Two or more alternations are executed in the long mordent.

The inverted mordent (♦) does not have the cross line. In it the lower auxiliary is replaced by the upper. It is the more commonly used mordent in music for the wind instruments.

The mordent takes its value from the principal note.

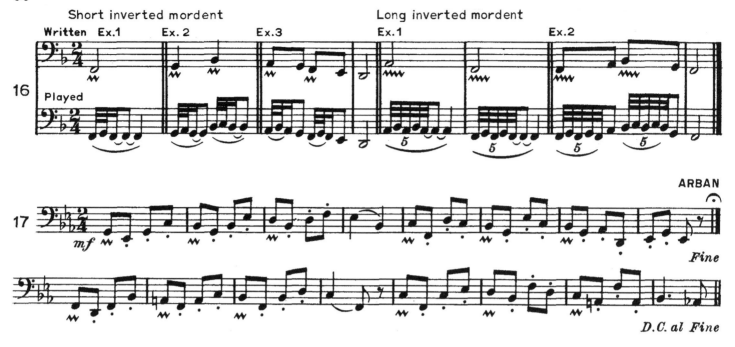

In trills of sufficient length a special ending is generally used whether indicated or not:

The closing of the trill consists of two tones: the scale tone below the principal note and the principal note.

In long trills of a solo character, it is good taste to commence slowly and gradually increase the speed. Practice the following exercises in the manner of both examples 1 and 2.

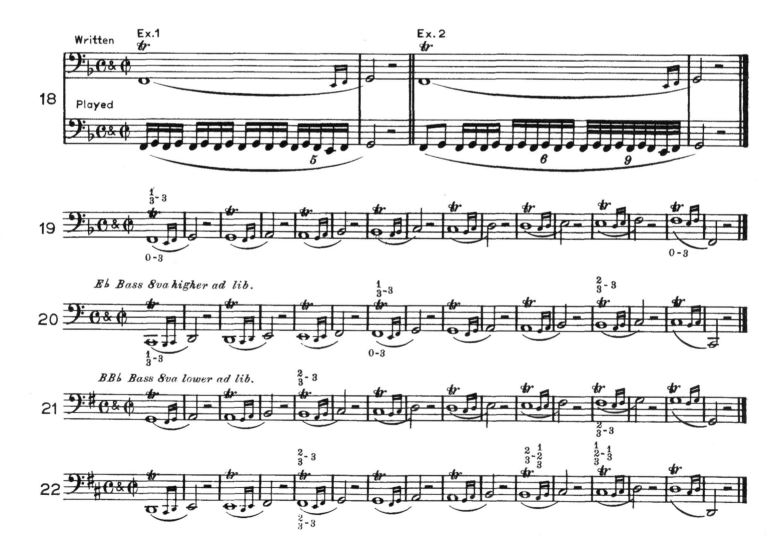

The Turn (Gruppetto)

The turn ∾ consists of four tones: the next scale tone above the principal tone, the principal tone itself, the tone below the principal tone, and the principal tone again.

When the turn is placed to the right of the note, the principal tone is held almost to its full value, then the turn is played just before the next melody tone. In this case (No.23, Exs. 1, 2, 3, 4, and 5) the four tones are of equal length.

When the turn is placed between a dotted note and another note having the same value as the dot (No.24, Exs. 1 and 3) the turn is then played with the last note of the turn taking the place of the dot, making two notes of the same value. The turn sign after a dotted note will indicate that one melody note lies hidden in the dot.

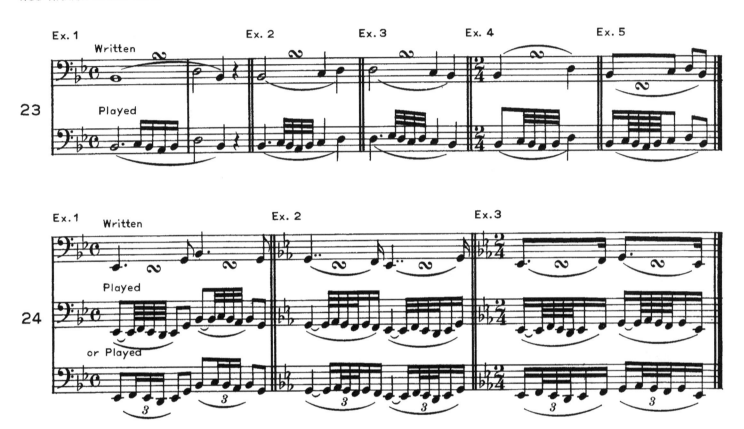

Sometimes an accidental sign occurs with the turn, and in this case when written below the sign, it refers to the lowest tone of the turn, but when written above, to the highest. (Exs. 1 and 2) below.

When the turn is placed over a note (Ex. 3) the tones are usually played quickly, and the fourth tone is then held until the time value of the note has expired.

In the inverted turn (Ex. 4) the order of tones is reversed, the lowest one coming first, the principal next, the highest third and the principal tone again, last. The inverted turn is indicated by the ordinary turn sign reversed ∾ or by ⊋.

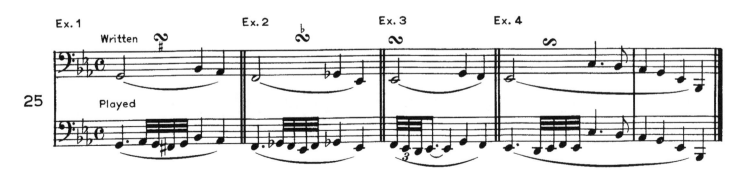

SOLOS
O Isis and Osiris
from "The Magic Flute"

MOZART

The Happy Farmer

SCHUMANN

Bourrée

HANDEL

Rule, Britannia

ARNE

Dio Possente
from "Faust"

GOUNOD

Spinning Wheel

ENDRESEN